Contents Table

Section 1:
Introduction to Computer Forensics

Welcome & What You'll Learn

Welcome to the exciting world of computer forensics! If you've ever been fascinated by the idea of uncovering hidden clues from digital devices, solving puzzles left behind in the wake of cybercrime, or simply want to understand how technology leaves indelible traces, then this book is for you.

The Digital Trailblazer's Guide

Computer forensics is a field that straddles the fascinating intersection between technology and investigation. It's the art and science of collecting, preserving, analyzing, and presenting digital evidence in a way that's both reliable and acceptable in legal settings. As our reliance on computers, smartphones, and the internet steadily increases, so too does the need for skilled professionals who can decipher the intricate digital trails we leave behind.

In this book, "Computer Forensics: Uncovering the Evidence – A Beginner's Guide to Investigating Digital Crimes," we'll embark on a knowledge-packed journey. Our goal is to equip you with a solid foundation in computer forensics and the techniques behind digital investigations.

What You Will Master

This book is meticulously structured to guide you from the fundamentals to the more intricate aspects of the field. Here's a glimpse into what awaits you:

- **The Foundations of Computer Forensics:** Understanding the very essence of computer forensics, its principles, different types of investigations it supports, and the meticulous processes used by professionals.

- **Delving into the Language of Data:** Grasping data encoding, deciphering hash files, and unraveling the complexities of hexadecimal representation.
- **Hardware and Filesystem Forensics:** Peeking under the hood to explore how the physical components of digital devices intertwine with file systems and operating systems, revealing forensically relevant information.
- **Imaging Techniques and Acquisition:** Mastering the tools of the trade—software used to capture and preserve pristine copies of digital evidence.
- **Image Mounting and Exploration:** Learning to navigate digital image files, unearthing a treasure trove of potential clues within them.
- **The First Responder's Role:** A practical guide on what to do (and importantly, what not to do!) when you are one of the first people on the scene of a potential digital crime.

Why Computer Forensics Matters

Computer forensics plays a pivotal role in our technological world. The skills you acquire can be employed across various spheres, including:

- **Law Enforcement and Criminal Investigations:** Assisting in solving a wide array of crimes, from cyber attacks and financial fraud to intellectual property theft and more.
- **Corporate Security:** Protecting organizations from data breaches, internal threats, and uncovering evidence in cases of employee misconduct.
- **Data Recovery for Individuals and Businesses:** Retrieving lost or accidentally deleted data, a crucial lifeline in the age of information.

Additional Resources to Deepen Your Learning

Throughout the book, I'll recommend valuable resources – websites, online tools, and communities where you can continue to broaden your knowledge and experiment with forensic techniques. Here are a few to get you started:

- **The Sleuth Kit:** https://www.sleuthkit.org/
- **The National Institute of Standards and Technology (NIST) Computer Forensic Tool Testing (CFTT) project:** https://www.nist.gov/itl/ssd/software-quality-group/computer-forensics-tool-testing-program-cftt

Let the Investigation Begin

By the end of this book, you'll gain the ability to think like a digital detective. Are you ready? Let's dive in and begin unraveling the intriguing world of computer forensics!

Deciphering Computer Forensics, Part 1

Welcome to the world of computer forensics! In the previous chapter, we set the stage, introducing you to this captivating field and outlining what lies ahead in this book. Now, it's time to delve deeper into the core concepts of what computer forensics truly encompasses.

What Exactly *IS* Computer Forensics?

Think of computer forensics as a blend of investigative science and digital detective work. At its heart, computer forensics involves:

- **Identifying Potential Evidence:** Locating digital data that might be relevant to an investigation – whether that's investigating a crime, an internal corporate incident, or perhaps just trying to recover lost files.
- **Preserving the Integrity of Evidence:** Taking meticulous steps to ensure that the original digital data remains absolutely unchanged and pristine. Any accidental modifications could ruin the evidence.
- **Analyzing the Evidence:** Using specialized tools and techniques to extract meaning from the raw data, piecing together clues, and forming conclusions.
- **Presenting Findings:** Clearly and accurately documenting the digital evidence and your analysis in a way that can be understood by others, such as attorneys, judges, company executives, or even a jury.

Computer Forensics: More Than Just Solving Crimes

While solving crimes is an important application of computer forensics, the field extends far beyond criminal cases. Here are just a few examples of the diverse scenarios where computer forensics comes into play:

- **Corporate Investigations:** Companies may use forensic techniques to investigate employee misconduct (e.g., data theft, harassment), policy violations, or to gather evidence in legal disputes.
- **Incident Response:** When a cyberattack or data breach occurs, computer forensics helps organizations identify how the breach

happened, what data might have been stolen, and what steps can be taken to prevent future incidents.

- **Recovery of Lost Data:** Even without malicious intent, files get deleted, hard drives fail, and data can seem lost forever. Forensic specialists often have the skills to recover this crucial information.
- **E-Discovery:** Within legal cases, digital evidence is increasingly important. Computer forensics plays a key role in collecting electronic documents, emails, and other forms of communication in the "discovery" phase of legal proceedings.

The Meticulous Forensic Process

Computer forensic investigations generally follow a structured approach to protect the integrity of evidence and ensure findings are reliable enough to be used in court (if needed). Let's outline the key phases:

1. **Identification:** Pinpointing where potential evidence might exist – hard drives, smartphones, servers in the cloud, etc.
2. **Preservation:** Creating exact copies of data while safeguarding the original evidence from any changes.
3. **Analysis:** Digging into the data with forensic tools, looking for deleted files, traces of web activity, suspicious changes to the system, and other clues.
4. **Documentation:** Thoroughly documenting every step of the process, from how evidence was collected to the techniques used to analyze it.
5. **Reporting:** Presenting the findings clearly, explaining their significance in the context of the broader investigation.

Important Principles to Keep in Mind

- **Chain of Custody:** It's vital to document every person who handles evidence and their actions. This ensures there's an unbroken record of accountability in case the evidence is challenged.
- **Admissibility in Court:** Not understanding forensic standards can jeopardize a case. Procedures and tools used must meet legal guidelines if the evidence is to be presented in court.

Further Resources

- **NIST Computer Forensics Reference Data Sets (CFReDS):** (https://www.cfreds.nist.gov/)
- **Computer Forensic Tool Testing (CFTT) project from NIST:** https://www.nist.gov/itl/ssd/software-quality-group/computer-forensics-tool-testing-program-cftt

Ready for Part 2?

Now that you have a solid understanding of the "what" and "why" of computer forensics, in the next chapter ("Deciphering Computer Forensics, Part 2"), we'll go deeper into the types of investigations, legal considerations, and the ethical responsibilities of computer forensic investigators.

Deciphering Computer Forensics, Part 2

In the previous chapter, we explored the fundamental concepts of computer forensics – what it is, the core investigative process, and the multitude of scenarios where it can be applied. Now, let's dive deeper into the different types of investigations a computer forensic expert might tackle, followed by the legal and ethical frameworks that guide the field.

Types of Computer Forensics Investigations

Within the overarching umbrella of computer forensics, there are several specializations and categories of investigations. Here are some of the most common types:

- **Criminal Investigations:** Arguably the most well-known, this branch supports law enforcement agencies investigating crimes where digital devices were involved. This includes cybercrime (attacks on computers, networks), fraud investigations, cases of intellectual property theft, and many others.
- **Civil Litigation:** Digital evidence plays an increasingly critical role in civil lawsuits. Forensic experts might assist in matters such as breach of contract disputes, employment violations, or even complex divorce proceedings where hidden assets could be involved.
- **Corporate Investigations:** Organizations often leverage computer forensics for internal investigations, such as suspected policy violations by employees, intellectual property theft, uncovering the source of a data breach, or gathering evidence for potential legal action against a competitor.
- **Data Recovery:** A core part of a forensic specialist's toolkit is the ability to recover accidentally or intentionally deleted files, sometimes even from damaged devices.
- **Security Incident Response:** When a cyberattack, hacking attempt, or data leak occurs, forensics plays a key role in understanding the scope of the breach, what data might be compromised, and how to prevent similar incidents in the future.

Navigating the Legal Landscape

Computer forensics is a field where technology and law intertwine. Investigators must operate within specific legal boundaries, especially when dealing with the collection, analysis, and presentation of evidence. Some of the key aspects to be aware of include:

- **Search and Seizure Laws:** Law enforcement, in most countries, must follow strict processes related to warrants and obtaining permission to seize digital devices for investigation.
- **Privacy Concerns:** There are laws governing what types of information are considered private, and how this may impact forensic investigations in different situations (criminal vs. corporate cases).
- **Chain of Custody:** We briefly touched on this in the previous chapter. Maintaining a clear, unbreakable chain of custody documenting who handles evidence and when is critical for the evidence to be admissible in court.
- **Preservation Orders:** In legal cases, courts can issue orders to preserve evidence and prevent its destruction (intentional or accidental) before it can be analyzed.

The Ethical Compass of Computer Forensics

Beyond legal requirements, computer forensic specialists have an ethical responsibility. This includes:

- **Neutrality:** Investigators should remain impartial throughout the case, focusing on the unbiased interpretation of the evidence.
- **Confidentiality:** Handling sensitive data, from private communications found on a device to corporate secrets, requires discretion and strict confidentiality.
- **Professional Competence:** Using accepted forensic methods, keeping skills up-to-date, and reporting on findings within the bounds of expertise.
- **Avoiding Conflicts of Interest:** If there's any situation that could compromise an investigator's impartiality, they should recuse themselves or make the conflict of interest clear at the outset.

The Evolving Nature of the Field

Technology, including devices, software, and how criminals operate, evolves rapidly. Computer forensic professionals must be lifelong learners to stay ahead of the curve. Some key challenges the field currently faces include:

- **Encryption:** The strong encryption found on many devices can make it difficult or impossible to access data, presenting challenges for investigators even when they have a legal right to do so.
- **The Cloud:** With more data stored on cloud servers scattered globally, obtaining evidence through traditional means becomes complex.
- **The Rapid Growth of Data:** The sheer volume of data stored on most personal and organizational devices can make investigations time-consuming and resource-intensive.

Additional Resources

- **The Digital Forensics Research Workshop (DFRWS):** (https://www.dfrws.org/)
- **Guidance Software: EnCase Forensic Resource page:** (https://www.guidancesoftware.com/encase-forensic)

Wrapping Up

In these two chapters, we've laid a strong foundation in the realm of computer forensics. Part 2 has shown how the field is much more than just crime-solving. Next, we'll begin exploring the technical core of forensics – starting with how computers store and represent data.

Section 2:
Delving into Data Encoding

Exploring Hash Files, Part 1

In the realm of computer forensics, hash files serve as unique digital fingerprints, crucial for several purposes that we'll explore in this chapter. Think of them as a kind of summary or compact code calculated based on the contents of a file. Let's unravel what hashing is, why it's important, and how it's used in digital investigations.

Understanding Hashes and Hash Functions

- **The Essence of a Hash:** A hash is a fixed-length string of numbers and letters (usually quite long) generated from a file, no matter the original file's size. It's like a unique barcode calculated from the raw data within that file.
- **Hash Functions:** These are mathematical algorithms that do the magic of transforming a file into a hash. Think of them as special code recipes that take a file as the ingredient and produce a hash as the output.
- **Key Properties**
  - **Uniqueness:** Two different files should almost never produce the same hash value - otherwise, we wouldn't have a reliable fingerprint.
  - **Unidirectional** You can't easily reverse-engineer a hash to get back the original file. (It's theoretically possible in specific cases, but extremely difficult for most forensic purposes).
  - **Sensitivity:** The tiniest change in the original file – even a single character – results in a drastically different hash value.

Common Hashing Algorithms

There are several well-established hash functions used in computer forensics and beyond. Some of the most popular ones include:

- **MD5 (Message-Digest Algorithm 5):** An older and widely used algorithm. While sufficient for some uses, the MD5 is now considered somewhat vulnerable to potential collisions (different files producing the same hash).
- **SHA-1 (Secure Hash Algorithm 1):** A more secure successor to MD5, though it, too, is gradually being phased out in favor of even stronger alternatives.
- **SHA-256 and SHA-512 (Secure Hash Algorithm 2):** Modern and robust algorithms, widely used for forensic and security applications. The '256' and '512' refer to the length of the hashes they produce.

Hash Files: Practical Applications in Forensics

Let's explore why hashes are incredibly valuable tools for computer forensic investigators:

1. **Verifying the Integrity of Data:**
   - Imagine you've made a copy of a suspect's hard drive. You calculate the hash of the original and the hash of the copy. If the hashes match, you have extremely strong proof that your copy is an *exact* duplicate.
   - This same principle applies for verifying files before and after transmission, ensuring they haven't changed in transit.
2. **Detecting File Tampering:**
   - Let's say a hacker tries to cover their tracks by modifying a log file. Recalculating its hash reveals a mismatch when compared to the original, raising a red flag for the investigator.
3. **Identifying Known Files Efficiently:**
   - Law enforcement and forensics teams maintain databases of known 'bad' files (e.g., containing malware). Instead of comparing entire files, hashes provide a fast way to identify if a suspicious file matches a fingerprint in the database.
   - This can also be used for categorizing files– identifying images even if their names have been changed, for instance.

Real-World Example

Imagine a case where child exploitation images are found on a suspect's computer. Using hashes, investigators can:

- Confirm their evidence image hasn't been altered since it was collected.
- Rapidly check if the illegal images match hashes of known images in law enforcement databases, confirming their content.

Additional Resources:

- **HashCalc (for Windows):** Software with a simple interface for calculating hashes: https://www.slavasoft.com/hashcalc/
- **NIST National Software Reference Library:** A repository of known software hashes: (https://www.nsrl.nist.gov/)

Coming Up in Part 2

In the next chapter, we'll go hands-on! I'll show you how to calculate hashes of files, explore more advanced uses of hashes in investigations, and consider limitations to be aware of.

Exploring Hash Files, Part 2

In the previous chapter, we laid the foundation for understanding hashes – what they are, popular algorithms used in forensics, and their core uses for verifying integrity and quickly identifying files. Now, let's get hands-on and explore some deeper applications of hash files.

Calculating Hashes: Tools of the Trade

Several tools (both specialized and general-purpose) can calculate hashes. Here's how to find them, and a few popular choices:

- **Forensic Suites:** Professional forensic software like EnCase, FTK, or Axiom will have built-in features for hashing files and often entire disk images.
- **Dedicated Hashing Tools:** Free programs like HashCalc (Windows) or dedicated command-line tools like md5sum, sha1sum (Linux/macOS) are designed specifically for hash calculations.
- **General File Verification Tools:** Some file management or compression software include an optional "checksum" feature, which is essentially calculating a hash to verify the file later.

Hands-On Exercise: Generating a Hash (choose one method)

We'll demonstrate with two common scenarios. Always note which algorithm (MD5, SHA-256, etc.) you used, as well as the resulting hash value.

- **Scenario 1: Dedicated Hashing Tool (e.g., HashCalc)**
    1. Download and install HashCalc.
    2. Open the software and find a file on your computer you want to practice on (text file, image, anything small for now).
    3. Select the hash algorithm you want to use (SHA-256 is a safe choice).
    4. Load the file into HashCalc.
    5. The calculated hash value will be displayed!
- **Scenario 2: Command-Line (Linux/macOS)**
    1. Open a terminal window.

2. **Use the cd command to navigate to the folder containing the file.** For example: `cd Documents`
3. **Use the appropriate command to calculate the hash:**
   - `md5sum filename.txt` (Replace 'filename.txt' with your actual file name)
   - `sha256sum filename.txt`

Advanced Use Cases for Hash Functions

Beyond basic file verification, hashes play roles in:

- **Identifying Malware:** Antivirus companies track hashes of known malware. Your computer can compare hashes of new files against these databases for rapid, low-resource-usage detection.
- **Deduplication in Big Data:** When storing massive datasets, hashes help quickly find identical files to reduce redundancy and save space.
- **Password Security:** Responsible websites never store your actual password. Instead, they store a hash of your password to check against when you log in.
- **Blockchain Technology:** Cryptocurrencies like Bitcoin use hashes extensively for linking 'blocks' of transactions, and as part of the "mining" process.

Are Hashes Foolproof? A Word on Collisions

While incredibly useful, hashes are *not* a magical bulletproof solution. Key things to understand about their limitations:

- **Collisions Are Possible, Just Rare:** Theoretically, different files *could* produce the same hash. With modern algorithms like SHA-256, it's *extremely unlikely* in forensic practice, but not impossible in the entire universe.
- **Hashes Detect Change, Not Malice:** A skilled adversary may modify a malicious file in a way that *intentionally* keeps the hash the same to evade basic detection.
- **Context Matters:** Relying solely on a file's hash being on a "bad" list is risky. Context clues from how and where the file was found will matter to an investigator.

Additional Resources

- **Learn about "Rainbow Tables":** A hacking attack using precalculated hashes for cracking passwords: (https://en.wikipedia.org/wiki/Rainbow_table)
- **Explore File Format Hashes:** (https://www.garykessler.net/library/file_sigs.html)

Wrapping Up

Hashes are surprisingly versatile, serving as the essential digital fingerprints in computer forensics. In the next chapter, we'll shift to another fundamental encoding concept – hexadecimal!

Demystifying Hexadecimal, Part 1

Get ready to dive into a world of 0s, 1s, letters, and the curious number system that computer forensic investigators need to understand – hexadecimal! While our everyday lives involve counting in groups of ten, computers fundamentally think in a language of two (binary). Hexadecimal offers a more human-friendly way to represent those binary patterns.

Why Do Computers Think in Binary?

At the very heart of it, computers operate using microscopic electronic switches that can be either on or off. We represent these two states as:

- '1' for an 'on' state
- '0' for an 'off' state

A single 'on'/'off' switch is called a bit. Groups of 8 bits form a byte – the basic building block for storing data in computers.

The Challenge of Reading Raw Binary

Imagine a forensic investigator having to interpret a long string of raw binary like this:

01001110 01101111 01110100 00100000 01100010 01101100 01101111 01101111 01101011

Deciphering this is tedious and very prone to error! This is where hexadecimal comes to the rescue.

Understanding Hexadecimal (Base-16)

Let's break down the word itself:

- 'Hexa' means six.
- 'decimal' refers to our usual base-10 counting system

Hexadecimal is a base-16 number system. This means it uses 16 unique symbols to represent numbers:

1. The digits 0 through 9 (their usual meaning)
2. Letters A through F (representing values 10 through 15)

Counting in Hexadecimal

Let's count from zero upwards to get a feel for it:

- Decimal: 0, 1, 2, 3, 4, ... 8, 9, 10, 11, 12 ...
- Hex: 0, 1, 2, 3, 4, ... 8, 9, A, B, C, ... F, 10, 11, 12 ...

Notice that in hexadecimal, we reach '10' after counting only to the symbol 'F'.

Hexadecimal's Advantage: Representing Binary

Each hexadecimal digit neatly maps to a group of 4 bits. Let's see a simple conversion table:

Decimal	Binary	Hexadecimal
0	0000	0
1	0001	1
2	0010	2
...	...	...
10	1010	A
11	1011	B
12	1100	C
...	...	...
15	1111	F

Real-World Example

Let's go back to that string of binary from earlier. Here's how it looks when converted to hexadecimal:

- **Binary:** 01001110 01101111 01110100 00100000 01100010 01101100 01101111 01101011
- **Hex:** 4E 6F 74 20 62 6C 6F 6B

It's much more compact and easier on the eyes!

Additional Resources

- **Khan Academy: Hexadecimal Introduction:** https://www.khanacademy.org/computing
- **RapidTables: Hexadecimal to Binary converter:** https://www.rapidtables.com/convert/number/hex-to-binary.html

In Part 2

We'll learn how to translate between hexadecimal, binary, and decimal. Plus, we'll explore where a forensic investigator is likely to encounter hexadecimal within digital evidence!

Demystifying Hexadecimal, Part 2

In the previous chapter, we introduced hexadecimal as a way to represent binary data in a more human-readable format. Now let's get comfortable with converting between the three fundamental number systems: decimal, binary, and hexadecimal.

Decoding the Number Systems

1. **Decimal (Base-10):** This is our everyday number system. Each digit's position has a value that's a power of ten (ones, tens, hundreds, etc.).
2. **Binary (Base-2):** The language of computers! Each digit's position represents a power of two (ones, twos, fours, eights, etc.).
3. **Hexadecimal (Base-16):** A shorthand for binary, where each digit maps to a group of four bits and positions are powers of sixteen (ones, sixteens, 256s, etc.).

Conversion Techniques

Decimal to Hexadecimal:

- **Division with Remainders:** Repeatedly divide the decimal number by 16. The remainders, read bottom to top, become your hexadecimal digits (remember to substitute A-F for remainders of 10-15).
- **Example:** Convert 215 (decimal) to hexadecimal
    - 215 / 16 = 13 remainder 7
    - 13 / 16 = 0 remainder 13 (D in hex)
    - Therefore, 215 (decimal) = D7 (hexadecimal)

Hexadecimal to Decimal:

- **Place Value:** Each position in the hexadecimal number represents a power of 16. Multiply each digit by its place value and add the results.
- **Example:** Convert CB (hexadecimal) to decimal
    - C (which is 12) * 16 = 192
    - B (which is 11) * 1 = 11

○ Therefore, CB (hexadecimal) = 203 (decimal)

Binary to Hexadecimal (and vice-versa)

- **This is the easiest!** Since each hexadecimal digit directly corresponds to 4 bits, simply group the binary into 4-bit chunks and use our conversion table from Part 1.

Practice Makes Perfect! (Exercise)

Try your hand at these conversions:

- Decimal 358 to Hexadecimal
- Hexadecimal A9 to Decimal
- Binary 10110101 to Hexadecimal

(Answers hidden for practice, highlight to view): [**Answers:** Decimal 358 = 166 Hex, A9 Hex = 169 Decimal, 10110101 Binary = B5 Hex]

Where You'll Encounter Hexadecimal in Forensics

A forensic investigator doesn't need to be a *hexadecimal wizard*, but it'll pop up frequently:

- **Raw disk views:** Software for examining the raw contents of a hard drive often displays data in hexadecimal.
- **File Headers:** Many file formats have specific starting bytes (a "magic number") that are identifiable by their hexadecimal representation.
- **Network Packet Analysis:** Captured network data packets are often analyzed in hexadecimal view for understanding data transmission protocols.
- **MAC Addresses:** The unique identifier for network adapters is a long hexadecimal number.
- **Memory Dumps:** When investigating malware or analyzing a running system's memory for clues, the investigator will see everything in hexadecimal.

Additional Resources

- **Hexadecimal Converter (for checking your work):**
  https://www.rapidtables.com/convert/number/hex-dec-bin-converter.html

Wrapping Up

The ability to understand and work with hexadecimal is a valuable addition to your computer forensics toolkit. As you delve deeper into investigations, you'll gain a natural intuition for this number system!

Section 3:
Unveiling Hardware and File Systems in Forensic Contexts

Hardware Probes: Unveiling Physical and Logical Copies, Part 1

In computer forensics, the starting point is often gathering a copy of data (from a hard drive, phone, etc.) to analyze. But how can we do this while ensuring the original evidence remains absolutely unchanged, and the copying process is forensically sound? Enter specialized tools known as hardware probes.

Why Direct Copies Often Aren't an Option

Here's the challenge that hardware probes solve:

- **Operating Systems Can Change Things:** If an investigator simply powers on a suspect computer and starts copying files, the very act of the OS running *modifies data.* System logs are updated, files may be moved, last access times change – potentially obscuring crucial evidence.
- **Protecting Fragile or Damaged Devices:** If a hard drive itself is failing or has potential hidden issues, the less interaction with it, the better. Forensic probes allow for copying with minimal strain on the original device.
- **Chain of Custody Needs:** To be admissible in court, evidence needs a clear record of who handled it, when, and what actions they took. Probes can incorporate documentation features.

Types of Hardware Probes

Let's look at two of the most common categories:

1. **Write Blockers**
   - **Purpose:** The core principle of computer forensics – never change the original evidence! Write blockers are placed *between* the suspect's storage device and the forensic analyst's computer.
   - **Functionality:** They allow data to be read from the source device but block *any* write commands sent toward the source. Think of them as a one-way shield.
   - **Types:** Write blockers can be hardware devices (e.g., Tableau blockers) or software-based (a feature in many forensic suites).

2. **Hardware Duplicators**
   - **Purpose:** To create a bit-for-bit exact copy of a storage device onto a target destination (another hard drive, for instance).
   - **Functionality:** These are standalone devices, independent of a computer. They efficiently copy data while bypassing the operating system and can often handle multiple copies simultaneously.
   - **Advanced Features:** Some duplicators include hashing (for on-the-fly verification of the copied data's integrity), and the ability to create copies using different formats (e.g., copying from an old IDE hard drive to a newer SATA drive).

Forensic Copying: Beyond Just a Copy

While the terms are sometimes used casually, there's a crucial distinction:

- **Physical Copy:** A complete replica of *all* data on the device, including deleted files, unallocated space, and hidden areas where potentially juicy evidence can lurk.
- **Logical Copy:** A copy of only the visible, active files and folders – like what a regular backup program might create.
- **Forensic Specialists Almost Always Want Physical Copies:** A logical copy *might* be sufficient for very simple cases, but if evidence is deleted, manipulated, or hidden, a physical copy is essential to reveal the whole picture.

Real-World Use Cases

Let's picture scenarios where hardware probes save the day:

- **Criminal Investigation:** A suspect's computer is seized. A write blocker is used, allowing investigators to safely preview the contents, boot from a forensics live CD for analysis, and create a physical copy — all without any changes to the original drive.
- **Corporate Data Breach:** A duplicator is used to quickly create copies of impacted employee laptops, minimizing downtime while preserving evidence.
- **E-discovery (Legal Context):** Hardware probes provide a defensible, documented method to collect and produce potentially relevant emails and business documents stored on devices.

Additional Resources

- **Digital Forensics Magazine - Using Hardware Write Blockers:** https://www.digitalforensicsmagazine.com/search?q=hardware+write+blockers
- **Forensic Focus - Write Blockers Article:** https://www.forensicfocus.com/tag/write-blockers/

Coming Up in Part 2

In the next chapter, we'll go deeper! We'll discuss scenarios where write blockers may not be suitable, and explore advanced techniques for dealing with encrypted devices and other challenges.

Hardware Probes: Unveiling Physical and Logical Copies, Part 2

In the previous chapter, we introduced write blockers and hardware duplicators as essential forensic tools. However, the world of digital evidence isn't always straightforward. Let's explore some scenarios where the choice of hardware tools and approaches gets more nuanced.

Scenarios Where Write Blockers Might Not Be Enough

While write blockers are invaluable, there are cases where they need to be used cautiously or combined with other strategies:

- **Encrypted Storage:** If a hard drive uses full-disk encryption, a traditional write blocker only protects against modifications at the hardware level. The contents will still be gibberish without the decryption key – special techniques may be needed.
- **Cloud Storage:** With data stored on remote servers (Dropbox, Gmail, etc.), write blockers won't help. Forensics here requires specialized tools and knowledge of how to preserve cloud-based evidence while working within the service provider's guidelines and legal requirements.
- **Mobile Devices (Phones & Tablets):** These devices often have built-in security features that prevent easy access even with a write blocker. Specialized mobile forensic tools may be needed to bypass passcodes or create a 'jailbroken' copy.
- **RAID Arrays:** Large storage systems often use multiple disks for redundancy or performance (RAIDs). Individual disks might not hold a meaningful copy. Special techniques are needed to capture the entire array at once.

Advanced Copy Techniques

Forensic specialists sometimes need to go beyond the core functions of a write blocker or duplicator. Here are a few examples:

- **Dealing with Bad Sectors:** A hard drive might have damaged areas (bad sectors) that are unreadable by normal means.

Forensic hardware and software might have 'skip' options or low-level read attempts to recover as much data as possible.

- **Targeted Logical Copies:** Sometimes only a specific subset of data is relevant, and time is of the essence. Tools might be used to create a logical copy of *only* email files, or documents from a certain time period, reducing the analysis scope.
- **Network Forensics:** Specialized probes capture live network traffic, often filtering to record only data relevant to the investigation. This is more about intercepting data in transit rather than copying a storage device.

Forensic Workstations: The Analyst's Toolkit

It's important to remember that a computer forensic analyst's setup is more than just hardware probes. They'll usually have:

- **Forensic Workstation:** A powerful computer isolated from the network, running specialized software. This is where forensic images are analyzed, and reports are generated.
- **Removable Drives:** Secure, write-protected storage for keeping evidence images and case notes.
- **Software Tools:** Forensic suites (EnCase, FTK, etc.) plus a multitude of smaller utilities that can analyze specific files, recover deleted data, crack passwords, and more.

Maintaining Professional Standards

Using hardware probes isn't just about the technical know-how. Forensic specialists adhere to strict guidelines to ensure their work is ethical and defensible in court:

- **Minimizing Interaction with Original Evidence:** The 'original' is often copied only once. If analysis requires another copy, it's usually made from the first copy, not the original device.
- **Documentation and Verification:** Every step – from acquiring evidence to analysis – is meticulously documented. Hashes are often used to prove copies remain identical to the source.
- **Accreditation and Training:** Many organizations offer certifications for forensic specialists, demonstrating their

understanding of hardware, software, and the governing procedures.

Additional Resources

- **Guidance Software: Handling Encrypted Drives:** (https://www.guidancesoftware.com/encase-forensic)
- **Forensic Focus – Mobile Device Forensics Article:** https://www.forensicfocus.com/tag/mobile-device-forensics/

Wrapping Up

The world of hardware probes is a blend of essential safeguards and adaptability in the face of complex scenarios. In the next chapter, we'll start shifting away from hardware, exploring how operating systems and file systems themselves are treasure troves of information for an investigator.

System Interactions: Exploring Hardware Devices, File Systems, and OS, Part 1

In this chapter, we'll begin dissecting how hardware, file systems, and operating systems (OS) interact, and the wealth of clues each layer can hold in a forensic investigation.

Think of a computer system like a complex, layered machine:

- **The Foundation: Hardware** – This is the physical base: hard drives, memory (RAM), the motherboard, graphics cards, and more.
- **The Organizer: File System** – The way files and folders are structured on a storage device, the rules for how they're named, stored, and retrieved.
- **The Brain: Operating System (OS)** – Software (like Windows, macOS, Linux) that manages the hardware, provides the interface for users, and runs applications.

A forensic investigator must understand how these layers work together because each can harbor important evidence.

Hardware: More Than Just Storage

Let's look beyond simply copying data from a hard drive. Here's what a deeper look at hardware might reveal:

- **Device Information:** Model numbers, serial numbers, manufacturer details – helpful to link devices to a suspect or a point of sale.
- **Network Connections:** MAC addresses of network cards and logs from wireless routers can show what networks the device connected to and when.
- **Peripherals:** Traces of connected USB drives, printers, or even deleted data from them might offer valuable leads.
- **Physical Damage or Alterations:** Signs of tampering could indicate attempts to destroy evidence or mask hardware components.

The File System: Mapping the Data Landscape

A file system is like a giant map and rulebook for the data on a storage device. Even *without* files, forensic clues lie within:

- **File Metadata:** Beyond a file's name and contents are timestamps (created, modified, last accessed). This can build a timeline of activity.
- **Deleted Files:** Often, 'deleted' files aren't truly erased from the disk – the file system just marks the space they occupied as available for overwriting. Forensic tools can often recover them.
- **Partitions:** A hard drive might have hidden or multiple partitions, each with its own file system, potentially attempting to conceal data.
- **Unallocated Space:** This is the "empty" area on the disk. Seemingly free space might contain fragments of old files, traces of web browsing, deleted documents, etc.

Common File Systems

A forensic investigator should be familiar with file systems used by popular operating systems:

- **Windows:** NTFS is the modern standard, older systems might have FAT32.
- **macOS:** Uses APFS (Apple File System), previously HFS+.
- **Linux:** Ext4 is the most widespread, others exist.
- **Mobile Devices:** Often use specialized file systems designed for flash memory.

The Operating System: A Treasure Trove

The OS is the heart of user interaction and software activity on a computer. Picking it apart can reveal:

- **System Logs:** Detailed records of system events, user logins, errors, hardware changes – a goldmine for tracing a user's actions.
- **Programs and Applications:** What's installed? Even the presence of file encryption or wiping tools can tell a story about a user's intent.

- **Web Browsing Artifacts:** Even if browsing history is cleared, caches, cookies, and remnants of downloads could expose the user's online activities.
- **Background Processes:** What's running at startup or hidden in the background? Forensic investigators look for signs of malware or tools used to obscure activity.

Challenges of Different Operating Systems

- **Windows:** The Registry is a central database of settings and activity, a complex but valuable source.
- **macOS:** While known for security, macOS still maintains detailed logs and has unique features like Time Machine backups.
- **Linux:** The sheer diversity of Linux flavors poses challenges, but the open-source nature can help analysis.

Additional Resources:

- **The Sleuth Kit wiki: File System Support Details:** https://wiki.sleuthkit.org/
- **NIST: Computer Forensic Reference Data Sets (CFReDS):** (https://www.cfreds.nist.gov/)

In Part 2

We'll dive deeper! We'll explore how file systems actually handle deletion and introduce some key operating system artifacts of immense interest to forensic investigators.

System Interactions: Exploring Hardware Devices, File Systems, and OS, Part 2

Let's delve further into recovering deleted data and examine valuable treasures within operating system artifacts!

File Deletion: The Illusion of Vanishing

When a user hits 'delete' on a file, what *actually* happens? In most cases:

1. **File Entry is Removed:** The file system directory (think of it as a table of contents) no longer shows the file's name or location.
2. **Space is Marked as Free:** The blocks on the disk where the file resided are now considered available for overwriting with new data.
3. **The File May *Linger*:** Unless overwritten, the raw data of the file often remains on the disk, invisible but potentially recoverable.

How Data Recovery Works (and Its Limits)

- **Forensic Tools Don't Just 'Undelete':** They scan unallocated space for recognizable file structures, looking for known headers and patterns indicative of images, documents, etc.
- **Success Isn't Guaranteed:** If the file was overwritten, there's little to be done. Solid State Drives (SSDs) complicate this even further due to how they manage data.
- **Fragments Tell a Partial Story:** Even recovering fragments of a file (parts of an image, pieces of a deleted email) could provide leads.

Key Operating System Artifacts for Investigators

Let's look at specific places forensics specialists look within a captured copy of an OS:

- **Windows Artifacts**
  - **The Registry:** A hierarchical database storing a wealth of system settings, user activity, recently opened files, USB device history, and more.

- **Jump Lists:** Those handy right-click menus on taskbar icons reveal recently accessed files of that type.
- **Prefetch Files:** Designed to improve app launch times, they can also expose programs the user ran and when.
- **Event Logs:** Security, System, and Application logs record an immense amount of detailed information on login events, errors, hardware changes, and more.

- **macOS Artifacts**
  - **Property Lists (plists):** XML files storing settings for applications and the system. Often contain recent activity trails.
  - **Spotlight Database:** Holds records of files and their metadata, sometimes even after the originals are deleted.
  - **Unified Logs:** A centralized log system with detailed records of system and application activities.

- **Linux Artifacts**
  - **Command-line History:** Bash history files (in a user's home directory) can show commands used over time.
  - **System Logs (often in /var/log):** A variety of logs track authentication attempts, process executions, kernel messages… the specifics depend on the Linux distribution.
  - **Hidden Files:** Many applications keep configuration or activity logs in hidden files (prefixed with '.') in a user's home directory.

The Challenge of Volume Shadow Copies

- **What It Is:** A Windows feature making periodic snapshots of files at a point in time.
- **Forensic Implications:**
  - **Potential Recovery Point:** May hold older versions of deleted files of interest to an investigator.
  - **Anti-Forensic Tool:** Suspects aware of forensics might intentionally *delete* files to wipe them from shadow copies, making recovery harder.

Additional Resources

- **SANS Institute Digital Forensics and Incident Response (DFIR) posters:** (https://www.sans.org/posters) – Great for visualizing common forensic artifacts
- **Forensic Wiki - Articles on specific artifacts:** https://forensicswiki.org/wiki/Main_Page

Wrapping Up

The interplay of hardware, file systems, and the OS leaves a remarkably detailed trace of activity. A computer forensic investigator, armed with knowledge of these artifacts and tools to recover seemingly lost data, can piece together a compelling narrative of events, crucial in any investigation.

Coming Up Next

In the next chapter, we'll delve into the world of forensic imaging software – the essential tools for capturing and preserving digital evidence in a forensically sound manner.

Section 4:
Exploring Imaging Techniques

Overview of Imaging Software, Part 1

In previous chapters, we've explored hardware probes for safeguarding evidence during acquisition and learned why operating with directly on the original is a major forensic no-no. This is where imaging software becomes indispensable. It allows investigators to create a forensically perfect duplicate, and then perform their analysis on the *copy*, leaving the original source untouched.

What Forensic Imaging Software Does

At its heart, imaging software does these crucial things:

1. **Bit-by-Bit Copy:** Creates an *exact* replica of a storage device (hard drive, USB stick, etc.). This includes deleted files, unallocated space, hidden areas – the whole picture.
2. **Verification with Hashes:** Calculates a hash value (e.g., SHA-256) of the original drive, and another hash of the created image. If the hashes match, this proves with extremely high reliability that the image is a faithful copy.
3. **Forensically Sound:** These tools interact with hardware using write-blocking features or operate within the parameters that ensure original evidence isn't altered in any way during the process.
4. **Image Format:** The resulting copy is usually saved in a special forensic image format. We'll cover these in more detail in Part 2.

Beyond Copying: Features of Forensic Software

The best imaging software doesn't just stop at basic cloning. Here are additional capabilities investigators rely on:

- **Dealing with Errors:** If a drive has bad sectors (damaged areas), advanced software may include options to attempt multiple reads or skip over unreadable areas while still capturing the maximum amount of data possible.

- **Selective Imaging:** Sometimes, creating a full physical image may be overkill. Tools might let you copy *only* specific file types or files from within a date range.
- **Compression:** Image files can get massive. Compression helps save space, although there's a trade-off of processing time to compress/decompress.
- **Encryption:** To safeguard sensitive case data, the forensic image itself might be encrypted, preventing unauthorized access.
- **Metadata and Notes:** Space is often included to document the who, what, when, and where of image acquisition, maintaining the chain of custody.

Popular Forensic Imaging Tools

The world of forensic software offers both commercial heavy-hitters and powerful open-source alternatives:

- **Commercial**
  - **FTK Imager (AccessData):** Industry standard, part of the full FTK forensics suite.
  - **EnCase Imager (Guidance Software):** Another forensics powerhouse, similar features to FTK Imager.
  - **X-Ways Forensics:** Comprehensive forensic solution including imaging capabilities.
- **Open Source**
  - **Guymager:** Well-respected free tool for Linux environments.
  - **dcfldd:** Command-line driven tool (enhanced version of the classic 'dd' command), favored by advanced users for flexibility.

Factors in Choosing Imaging Software

Forensic specialists consider the following when selecting tools for their toolkit:

- **Supported File Formats:** Can it handle the various image formats you'll encounter (covered in Part 2!) and any proprietary formats?

- **Evidence Types:** Does it support hard drives, SSDs, mobile devices, and more?
- **Ease of Use vs. Flexibility:** GUI-based tools are easier for beginners, command-line ones offer more power to experts.
- **Reporting Features:** How easily can you generate case documentation and include it within the image or as a separate file?

Additional Resources

- **NIST Software Reference Library (includes disk imaging tools):** (https://www.nsrl.nist.gov/)
- **Forensic Focus article comparing imaging tools:** https://www.forensicfocus.com/tag/imaging-tools/

In Part 2

We'll go deeper into common forensic image formats, what makes them special, and the considerations involved when choosing which format to use for a case.

Overview of Imaging Software, Part 2

In the previous chapter, we discussed the core functions and features of forensic imaging tools. Now, let's explore the specialized file formats they use to store the all-important forensic duplicates. Understanding these isn't just technical trivia – the choice of format has real-world implications for an investigation.

Why Special Image Formats?

Forensic image formats aren't like your typical .jpg or .zip files. They have unique requirements:

- **Capturing Everything:** They must store not just files, but raw disk structure, deleted data, metadata, potentially even unallocated space.
- **Verification:** Often, mechanisms for storing the hash value are built-in to the format, ensuring image integrity.
- **Space for Notes:** Case details, imaging logs, and chain of custody info can be embedded within the image file itself.
- **Tool Compatibility:** While some formats are open, others are proprietary to specific forensic software.

Common Image Formats

Let's look at some of the major players in the world of forensic images:

1. **Raw (dd)**
   - **The Basics:** The most basic format, a sector-by-sector copy, no fancy features.
   - **Pros:** Simple, fast, universally compatible.
   - **Cons:** No built-in compression, hash verification, or metadata storage. Files can be HUGE.
2. **Advanced Forensic Format (AFF)**
   - **Open-Source Standard:** Designed specifically for forensics, strikes a balance of features and cross-compatibility.
   - **Pros:** Supports compression, internal hash storage, metadata, and can be split into multiple segments.
   - **Cons:** Slightly less common than raw, some older tools might not support it.
3. **Expert Witness Format (E01)**

- **Linked to EnCase:** EnCase software's format, the industry standard for a long time.
- **Pros:** Supports compression, multiple segments, the ability to add external notes.
- **Cons:** Proprietary format, so less compatibility with non-EnCase tools.

Considerations When Choosing a Format

A forensic investigator doesn't just pick any format – the decision depends on:

- **Compatibility with Analysis Tools:** Will the format be easily usable with the forensic suite you intend to use for analyzing the evidence?
- **Storage Capacity:** If space is a concern, compressed formats (AFF, E01) are better, but might slightly slow down processing.
- **Court Admissibility:** While less of an issue now, in some jurisdictions raw (dd) was seen as more 'trustworthy' in the past due to its simplicity.
- **Need for Metadata:** Do you need to embed ample notes and case information directly into the image?

Beyond the Big Three

While we focused on the most prevalent formats, be aware that:

- **Other Vendors Have Their Formats:** X-Ways has its own, so do other tools. This sometimes limits compatibility.
- **Virtual Machine Images:** When acquiring images of full virtual machines (VMs), the image might be in VMWare's VMDK format or similar, representing multiple virtual hard disks.

Rarely Just a Single Image

It's important to understand that, in practice, investigators may make multiple images:

- **Initial Acquisition:** A raw (dd) image might be made for its simplicity and guaranteed compatibility.

- **Working Copy:** A conversion to AFF or E01 might happen for the compression and metadata features when preparing for analysis.

Additional Resources

- **Digital Forensics Wiki - Disk Image Formats:**
  https://forensicswiki.org/wiki/Disk_image_format
- **AFF4 Project (Advanced Forensic Format standard):**
  (https://github.com/aff4)

Wrapping Up

The ability to create forensically sound images, and understanding the strengths and weaknesses of different image formats, is crucial for any digital evidence investigator.

Up Next

Now that you grasp imaging concepts, we'll move onto the practical process of *acquiring* that image in a secure and forensically sound way!

Section 5:
Forensic Image Acquisition

Crafting a Digital Snapshot: Crafting a Forensic Disk Image, Part 1

Let's get hands-on! In this chapter, we'll begin the process of crafting a forensic disk image. Remember, our goal is safeguarding the original evidence while creating a perfect copy to investigate.

Preparation is Key

Before touching any evidence, meticulous preparation ensures a successful process and defensible results:

1. **Documentation Forms:** Have ready templates to record EVERY action – dates, times, hardware serial numbers, who had custody, software used, the hash of the original device, the hash of the resulting image, etc.
2. **Forensically Clean Workstation:** This computer is dedicated to analysis, isolated from networks, and running trusted forensic software.
3. **Write Blocker:** Verify your hardware write blocker (or software equivalent if built into your forensic suite) is functioning correctly.
4. **Storage for the Image:** Prepare a secure hard drive, ideally exceeding the size of the target drive. This target could also be a network share, depending on your lab's setup.
5. **Imaging Software of Choice:** Be familiar with your tool (FTK Imager, Encase, command-line tools, etc.). Know the settings, where to store log files, and the image format you'll use.

The Imaging Workflow (General Overview)

While tools have their variations, the core steps usually are:

1. **Connect the Evidence Device:** With the write blocker in place, attach the suspect's drive to your forensic workstation. Document which ports, cables, etc. were used!
2. **Capture Drive Information:** BEFORE creating the image, your software should let you record the drive's make, model, serial number, and any existing partitions or visible file system details.
3. **Start the Imaging Process:** The software will guide you to choose the source drive (the evidence), destination location (where to save the image file), image format, and hash calculation options.
4. **Hash Verification:** Once the image is fully created, the MOST important step. Your tool COMPARE the calculated hash of the image against the hash of the original drive. They MUST match.
5. **Documentation, Documentation!** Fill out your forms meticulously. Any gaps here can undermine your entire case if it ever goes to court.

Real-World Complications: It's Rarely This Simple

Let's address some scenarios that make imaging more interesting:

- **Encrypted Drives:** If the drive has full-disk encryption, your traditional image will be useless until decrypted. This may need specialized tools, court orders to obtain a password, or brute-forcing attempts.
- **Damaged Drives:** When the drive itself has physical problems, you'll need specialized hardware/software that can do error handling and multiple read attempts to maximize recovery of salvageable data.
- **Massive Drives:** Imaging a multi-terabyte drive takes time. Some tools let you 'pause' the process and resume if needed.
- **Raids or Unusual Setups:** Network Attached Storage, complex servers – sometimes a simple, single hard drive image is not the answer, and a full understanding of the system's configuration is necessary.

Additional Resources

- **SANS Digital Forensics – Cheat Sheet for Imaging Process:** https://www.sans.org/security-resources/posters/digital-forensics-imaging-process/
- **NIST Computer Forensics Tool Testing Program: Disk Imaging Tools:** https://www.cftt.nist.gov/disk_imaging.htm

In Part 2

We'll go deeper into potential error scenarios, additional types of forensic images (like imaging a live system's RAM), and look at tools for imaging smartphones and other mobile devices, which have their own set of challenges.

Crafting a Digital Snapshot: Crafting a Forensic Disk Image, Part 2

In the previous chapter, we covered the basics of forensic imaging. Now let's address the wrinkles and complexities that make every case unique.

Error Handling: When Things Don't Go Smoothly

- **Bad Sectors:** If the drive itself is damaged, your software may encounter errors reading certain areas. Advanced tools have options like:
    - **Multiple Read Attempts:** Retry difficult sectors several times.
    - **Skipping Errors:** If data is truly unrecoverable, proceed but log the bad sectors for later analysis.
    - **Hashing Each Sector:** Provides proof of the *exact* state of the copy, even if unreadable areas exist.
- **Power Outages/Accidental Disconnects:** If imaging is interrupted unexpectedly, DO NOT just try again. Assess the state of the image file (may be corrupt), log the incident fully, and potentially start the acquisition from scratch.

Beyond Hard Drives: Other Image Types

- **Live System Imaging:** Sometimes capturing the RAM (memory) of a running computer is essential. This shows running processes, network connections, etc., which would be lost on shutdown. It requires specialized tools.
- **Logical Imaging:** If only certain files or a single partition are relevant, logical images are smaller and faster, but they miss deleted data and unallocated space.
- **Targeted Imaging:** Software may allow copying *just* email files, or documents modified within a certain timeframe, to shorten analysis time.

Forensic Imaging of Mobile Devices

Smartphones and tablets pose unique hurdles:

- **No Easy Drive Removal:** They can't often be connected like external hard drives. Specialized mobile forensic tools/equipment are necessary.
- **Security & Encryption:** Bypassing lockscreens, dealing with full device encryption might involve 'jailbreaking' techniques or obtaining warrants to compel passcodes.
- **Variety is Immense:** Each OS version, device model can have quirks, requiring the investigator to be continually learning.
- **Data Beyond the 'Filesystem':** Apps often keep their own data stores, requiring the use of app-specific extraction tools to make sense of them.

Network Forensics & Cloud Considerations

- **Network Packet Capture:** Special tools "sniff" data as it flows over the network, making a copy of traffic for later analysis. This isn't disk imaging in the traditional sense, but similar principles of unaltered preservation apply.
- **Cloud Image? Often Not Feasible:** With data in cloud services (Gmail, Dropbox), acquiring a traditional disk image is impossible. This usually involves working through the service provider, legal requests (warrants), and their internal preservation tools.

Specialized Scenarios: A Few Examples

- **Deleted File Recovery On Solid State Drives (SSDs):** Due to how SSDs manage data, even standard forensic imaging might not fully recover deleted files. Highly specialized techniques and tools might be necessary.
- **Virtual Machine Images:** Forensic analysis of the entire virtual system requires imaging the virtual hard disk files (VMDK or similar), along with the host system's configuration.
- **Anti-Forensics: Wiping Tools & 'Burner' Devices:** Suspects savvy enough to use data wiping tools leave fewer traces. Investigators then focus on system logs, fragments left behind by wiping tools, or even hardware analysis.

Documentation is Your Lifeline!

Especially when complications arise, these underline the importance of rigorous documentation:

- **Why That Image Type?:** Justify the choice of live image vs. physical.
- **Record Any Errors:** They may provide clues or require expert follow-up.
- **The Limits of Your Tools:** Software failing to extract texts from a certain app shouldn't end your investigation, it should be a well-documented limitation.

Additional Resources

- **Forensic Focus on Mobile Forensics:** https://www.forensicfocus.com/tag/mobile-forensics/
- **Cellbrite (Major Mobile Forensic Tool Vendor):** https://www.cellebrite.com/en/home/

Wrapping Up

Forensic image creation is part science, part meticulous process, and the ability to adapt to the unpredictable. With a solid foundation in the core principles, and an understanding of the variety of tools and techniques out there, an investigator is well-equipped to preserve that precious digital evidence.

Integrating Evidence: Incorporating Additional Elements

The beauty of computer forensics is how disparate pieces of data weave together a story. While we've focused on capturing pristine disk images, understand that they never exist in a vacuum. Let's explore other sources to consider, and how they complement the information extracted from an image.

Types of Supplemental Evidence

1. **Network Logs & Artifacts**
   - **Firewall/Router Logs:** If a crime involves online activity, logs from network hardware might show destination IP addresses, times of access, and hint at websites or services used.
   - **Proxy/VPN Logs:** If the suspect tried to mask their online activity, logs from proxy or VPN providers (if obtainable by legal process) can expose the real source of the traffic.
   - **Wireless Network Records:** Connection logs from WiFi access points might tie a suspect's device to a physical location and time window.
2. **Cloud & Service Provider Data**
   - **Email Providers:** With legal warrants, investigators can obtain archived emails, sent/draft folders, contact lists, and metadata, even if a suspect deleted them locally.
   - **Social Media:** Even deleted posts and messages can sometimes be recovered from service providers, often containing revealing communication.
   - **Cloud Storage (Dropbox, etc.):** Document versions, deleted files, and access logs provide timelines of activity.
   - **ISPs (Internet Providers):** Subscriber records can link an IP address back to an individual or organization.
3. **Physical Evidence from the Scene**
   - **Other Devices:** Was there a USB thumb drive plugged in, smartphones nearby, a printer connected? Each of these could hold relevant data.

- ○ **Hardware Examination:** Tool marks on a computer case, unusual wiring, or modifications can offer clues about a suspect's technical savvy.
  - ○ **Documents:** Printed files, handwritten notes, passwords scribbled on sticky notes – the 'old-fashioned' stuff shouldn't be overlooked!
4. **Witness Statements & Suspect Interviews**
   - ○ **Non-Technical Information:** Witnesses can place the suspect near the computer, observe odd behavior, or provide context to technical findings.
   - ○ **Passwords & Usernames:** If devices are secured, obtaining these from the suspect (voluntarily or compelled) could save the time-consuming and sometimes impossible task of cracking them.

Combining Evidence Sources: Case Examples

Let's illustrate how integration is crucial:

- **Child Exploitation Case:**
  - ○ **Image Analysis:** Reveals illicit images on the hard drive
  - ○ **Browser History:** Shows what websites the suspect frequented
  - ○ **Cloud Storage:** **Uncovers a hidden backup folder filled with more content.
  - ○ **ISP Records:** Tie the computer's internet usage to the timeframe of uploads, possibly identifying online distribution of the material.
- **Financial Fraud Case:**
  - ○ **Image Analysis:** Locates a cleverly hidden spreadsheet of fake transactions.
  - ○ **Email Records:** Provides communication with co-conspirators discussing the money flow.
  - ○ **Physical Documents:** Receipts found at the scene correlate with dates and amounts in the scheme.

The Challenge of Timelines

One of the trickiest, yet most potent, aspects of forensic integration is building timelines:

- **Syncing Clocks:** Is the computer clock accurate? Did the suspect change timezones? Correlating this with logs from external sources is vital.
- **File Timestamps:** Created/modified timestamps can be manipulated. Tools can help determine if file timestamps are consistent or show anomalies.
- **Data from Multiple Devices:** Overlapping usage of a laptop, a phone, and actions captured by online service logs helps pinpoint what a person was doing, and when.

Additional Resources

- **NICE Framework - Areas of Cyber Investigative Knowledge:** A helpful way to visualize everything involved in cybercrime forensics https://www.nist.gov/itl/applied-cybersecurity/nice/nice-cybersecurity-workforce-framework
- **Computer Crime & Intellectual Property Section (CCIPS) - U.S Dept. of Justice:** https://www.justice.gov/criminal-ccips

Wrapping Up

Forensic investigations are like puzzles, with the disk image being a major piece, but rarely the complete solution. By understanding the potential additional evidence sources and how to tie them together, a forensic analyst moves from simply recovering data to reconstructing events, motives, and the identities of those involved.

Section 6:
Mounting and Exploration of Digital Images

Ascending the Digital Peak: Mounting a Digital Image

In this chapter, we'll tackle the art of mounting a forensic image. Think of it as the crucial gateway to safely exploring the evidence within. So far, you've mastered safeguarding evidence via imaging. That alone, though, is like possessing a treasure chest without a key. Let's dive into mounting to 'unlock' the image and begin our analysis.

Why Mount an Image?

Let's reiterate why we don't simply start poking around the raw forensic image file:

- **Risk of Alteration:** Forensic tools must never risk modifying the original evidence, so your image is 'sacred'.
- **User-Friendly Interface:** Raw images in DD or E01 formats aren't designed to be browsed like normal files. Mounting makes them readable.
- **Integration with Forensic Tools:** Specialized forensic software expects a mounted disk image to work its magic, performing deep searches, timeline analysis, etc.

The Mechanics of Mounting

There are two primary ways to mount a forensic image:

1. **Physical Write-Blocker + Image Mount:**
   - **The 'Classic' Way:** Using a hardware write-blocker, you connect the *actual forensic image drive* (the one containing the copy of data) to your forensic workstation.

- ○ **Mounting Software:** Tools within your forensic suite (FTK Imager, Encase, etc.) can then mount partitions within the image as if they were separate drives.
2. **Virtual Mounting**
    - ○ **Software Does the Work:** There might be no additional physical drive involved. The software presents the content of the image file as a virtual drive within your operating system.
    - ○ **Advantages:** Can be faster to set up, especially if an image is already stored on your workstation's hard drive or a network share.

Exploring a Mounted Image

Once mounted, what you'll see depends on several factors:

- **Image Type:**
    - ○ **Full Disk Image:** You'll likely see all partitions as if the original hard drive was connected (C:\ drive, hidden recovery partitions, etc.).
    - ○ **Logical Image:** Only the specific folder or partition imaged will be exposed.
- **The Forensic Tool:**
    - ○ **Familiar File Browser:** Some tools present a familiar Explorer-like interface (in read-only mode!) within the forensic software itself.
    - ○ **Disk Management View:** Others may resemble Windows Disk Management, aiming to give a sense of the original disk layout.

Caveats & Considerations

- **Not All File Systems Are Equal**: Your tools may perfectly handle mounting images with Windows (NTFS), but stumble with MacOS (APFS) or Linux file systems.
- **Encryption is Still a Barrier:** If the original disk was encrypted, the mounted image will be too, until it's decrypted.
- **The Illusion of 'Normalcy'**: While mounted, it's easy to forget you're looking at a copy. Resist the urge to run programs within, right-click, or perform actions meant for a normal hard drive.

Forensic 'Swiss Army Knives'

Some forensic suites offer incredible flexibility in *how* they mount images, which is useful for advanced analysis:

- **Mounting Individual Files:** Need to parse a single PST (Outlook Email), database, or a browser history file? Tools may let you mount them in isolation, without the entire disk structure.
- **Read-Only vs. Limited Write Access:** Some software may allow mounting in a special mode, logging any file access attempts by your forensic tools. This becomes very useful during live system analysis.

Additional Resources

- **X-Ways Forensics: Image Mounting Concepts:**
  https://www.x-ways.net/forensics/

Wrapping Up

Mounting a forensic disk image marks a milestone: the shift from evidence preservation to hands-on exploration. Now that you understand the process and its nuances, the next step is uncovering the secrets lying within the image itself!

Exploring the Digital Image, Part 1

With your forensic image mounted, it's tempting to start clicking around at random. Resist! A methodical approach ensures you don't miss crucial information and that your findings will be organized for reporting later.

The Art of Forensic Search

Forensic analysis of an image has different goals from casual browsing or even tech support:

- **You're Not Just Fixing Things:** It's more about finding traces of *what* happened on the computer, *when*, and potentially *who* was involved.
- **Thoroughness Is Key:** You often can't assume a suspect nicely organized incriminating data for you. A relevant file might be misnamed, deleted, or fragmented.
- **Context Matters:** A single suspicious image is less telling than the same image found alongside a web browser cache showing related search terms and a deleted document draft discussing its creation.

Where to Begin? A High-Level Plan

1. **Case Specifics Drive Your Focus:** Are you looking for evidence of financial fraud, specific illegal content, or traces of hacking activity? This shapes your search strategies.
2. **Start with the Familiar:** Focus first on 'normal' user files on the image – documents, images, the email inbox, etc. These are most likely to yield understandable clues.
3. **Leverage OS Artifacts:** We'll dedicate an entire chapter to these treasures, but start by understanding where the operating system logs its activity, and get comfortable with the file systems.

Forensic Software: Your Toolkit

The right tools are your loyal companions in image exploration. Key features include:

- **Keyword Searching:** Searching within the image across *all* files (including deleted ones) for terms relevant to your case is essential.
- **Timeline Creation:** Software aids in building a timeline of file creation, modification, and access with the image as the data source.
- **Filtering:** Focus in on certain file types (e.g., only show JPG images), or files within a specific date range.
- **Deleted File Recovery:** Exploring free space and file system structures to attempt bringing back deleted data.
- **Hash Matching:** Comparing files within the image against databases of known good (e.g., Windows system files) or known bad (e.g., illegal content) files.

First Steps with a Mounted Image

Let's imagine a scenario for a simple example:

Case Scenario: Suspicion of an employee leaking company secrets

Initial Exploration:

- **Locations of Interest:** Start with the user's "My Documents" folder, desktop, recent document lists within programs, and sent email folders.
- **Search Keywords:** Company name, project code-names, competitor names, words like "confidential" or "leak".
- **Check Image Metadata:** Even deleted files might reveal creation dates or software used, offering leads.

Additional Resources

- **Autopsy Forensic Browser (Free and Open-Source):** https://www.autopsy.com/
- **Guidance Software: Encase Forensic User Docs:** https://www.guidancesoftware.com/encase-forensic
- **Forensic Focus Article - Search Techniques:** https://www.forensicfocus.com/tag/search-techniques/

Practical Considerations

Real forensic analysis is often…

- **Time-Consuming:** Large disk images take time to process and search through.
- **Repetitive:** You might run multiple search variations, tweaking keywords, and refining the scope.
- **Collaborative:** A complex case may involve specialists for different file types or OS artifacts.

In Part 2

We'll go deeper, focusing on those treasure troves of forensic information – the traces left behind by the operating system itself. We'll look at what they tell us about the user's actions!

Exploring the Digital Image, Part 2

Let's continue our journey into forensic image analysis. In this chapter, we'll uncover how the OS logs a wealth of actions, creating an incredibly valuable timeline for your investigation!

The Treasure Trove of OS Artifacts

Every action on a computer leaves a digital footprint somewhere within the operating system. Key areas for your investigation become:

- **Windows Artifacts**
  - **The Registry:** A massive database holding configurations and activity trails. Recent documents, USB device plug-in history, program associations, and much more are recorded here.
  - **Event Logs:** Security events, errors, logins – a structured record of system-level occurrences.
  - **Jump Lists & Prefetch:** Designed to help applications start faster, these reveal what the user ran, and when.
  - **Browser Artifacts:** History, cache, cookies… a suspect's web activity is often meticulously logged.
- **macOS Artifacts**
  - **System Logs:** Stored in various places depending on the OS version, they track process launches, authentication events, and more.
  - **Property Lists (plists):** Configuration files for applications, these reveal usage patterns.
  - **Spotlight Database:** Files indexed as searchable, potentially exposing items even if deleted from their original location.
- **Linux Artifacts**
  - **Variety Is the Spice:** Due to different Linux flavors (Ubuntu, etc.), log locations aren't as standardized. Key places include /var/log, and user-specific logs in their home directories.
  - **Command-line History:** Tells you what a user executed in the terminal. Incredibly revealing for skilled users.

Forensic Tools Become Your Friend

Manually combing through OS artifacts is a headache! Forensic tools provide features to parse, present, and search these artifacts in a human-friendly way. They become adept at:

- **Timeline Creation:** Correlating timestamps from multiple artifact types to create a single, detailed timeline of actions on the system.
- **Registry Analysis:** Dedicated registry viewers make it easier to explore the complex structure of the Windows registry.
- **Web Browser Artifact Viewers:** Present browsing history, bookmarks, etc., in a familiar way, even recovering deleted items sometimes.

Example: Putting the Pieces Together

Let's revisit our "leaked company data" scenario from the previous chapter. Key analysis steps would be:

1. **Building a Timeline:**
   - Registry keys with USB devices plugged in and their last timestamps
   - Browser history and file timestamps around visits to cloud storage or competitor websites
   - Timestamps on suspected leaked files themselves, if those exist on the image.
2. **Focusing Search Terms with Context:**
   - Search not ONLY for project names but combine those terms with dates revealed by the timeline. This reduces the noise of unrelated old documents turning up.
3. **Examining System Logs:**
   - Unusual timestamps of system boot-ups (did the employee work late?)
   - Errors or log entries related to file archiving tools (WinZip, 7-zip, etc.), which might be used to package data for exfiltration.

Important Caveats

OS Artifacts tell a story, but it's not always complete:

- **Anti-Forensics:** Suspects savvy enough to wipe traces might erase log entries or manipulate timestamps. This itself can be a clue!
- **Encryption:** If certain files or the whole drive is encrypted, you might face access hurdles despite the artifacts clearly pointing to their existence.
- **The Limits of Logging:** Not every action is guaranteed to be logged, especially very specialized activity or malware that tries to stay under the radar.

Additional Resources

- **Belkasoft Blog on Analyzing Artifacts:** https://belkasoft.com/blog
- **SANS Digital Forensics Poster (shows common artifact locations):** https://www.sans.org/posters

Wrapping Up

Forensic analysis of an image is the combination of searching for specific files but also understanding what the operating system logs reveal about the bigger picture.

Up Next

Sometimes, the most crucial evidence isn't from the primary suspect's device. We'll look at the crucial role of first responders in the digital forensics process – those who arrive on the scene before a dedicated analyst does.

Section 7:
First Responder Assistance

First Responders' Guide to Evidence Collection, Part 1

Let's shift our focus to those who play a crucial role in digital investigations - the first responders. These are often police officers, private security personnel, or incident responders within a company who are first on the scene of a potential crime or policy violation.

Why First Responders Matter in Digital Forensics

You might picture a 'CSI' type swooping in with high-tech tools, but the reality is this: the initial actions taken (or NOT taken) by first responders can make or break the entire investigation.

- **The Fragility of Digital Evidence:** Unlike a bloody weapon left at the crime scene, digital traces are easily *changed*. A simple act of turning a computer off incorrectly can destroy valuable data.
- **Chain of Custody Begins from the FIRST Touch:** A core legal principle. Whoever handles the evidence first establishes the all-important chain of custody, including documenting their actions in detail.
- **Scene Assessment is Key:** A responder noticing a blinking router light, or a discarded USB stick, provides leads that a forensic lab analyst arriving days later wouldn't have.

Core Principles for First Responders

Your goal IS NOT to become a full-blown forensic expert. Instead, it's crucial to remember these:

1. **Preserve, Preserve, Preserve:** The overriding priority is preventing further modification of potential evidence. When in doubt, do less!

2. **Document Everything:** *Who* did *what*, *when*, and *why*. Note the precise state in which you found the scene (computer was on, screen showed a suspicious error, etc.). Photos and sketches can be invaluable.
3. **Isolate the Network:** If a machine is on and connected, prevent it from communicating outwards if possible. This stops both potential further harm and remote data deletion.
4. **Identify Potential Evidence:** Don't just focus on the computer itself. Are there phones, tablets, external drives, USB keys, paper notebooks nearby… these might all be part of the picture.
5. **When in over Your Head, Ask for Help:** No shame in calling in specialists early. Some situations are just too complex or sensitive to risk doing the wrong thing.

"Digital" Crime Scenes Are Varied

First responders must adapt their approach based on the situation:

- **Corporate Policy Violation:** Here, your company likely has procedures, likely less strict than law enforcement. Focus is often on the user's computer and company-owned devices.
- **Suspected Child Exploitation:** Highest urgency, often strict protocols exist to minimize device interaction and to prioritize immediate action.
- **Hacking Incident:** If systems are still compromised, there's a balance between preservation and preventing further damage. This almost always needs specialists involved ASAP.
- **Physical Crime with Digital Traces:** Let's say a robbery where the suspect's phone is left behind. Even if your main focus is securing the physical scene, treat potential digital devices with extra care.

Basic Actions for Common Device Types

Let's get practical. If you MUST take some action before the forensic specialists arrive:

- **Desktop Computers (powered on):**
    - Photograph the screen content

- ○ Carefully disconnect the network cable (back of the machine)
- ○ IF possible, a trained responder can make a quick 'live' triage image of the RAM, which is very volatile.
- ○ If instructed to shut down, do so normally through the OS menu.
- **Desktop Computers (already off):**
  - ○ Do not turn them on.
  - ○ Document cables connected (what's plugged in where), take photos.
  - ○ Secure the entire computer.
- **Laptops (powered on):**
  - ○ Similar to desktops, focus on photographing the screen, network isolation, potential RAM capture if trained to do so.
  - ○ Shutdown is trickier due to the battery. Seek guidance if possible, as the best option may vary depending on circumstances.
- **Phones & Tablets:**
  - ○ If on, place them into airplane mode, or if possible, into a Faraday bag (signal-blocking).
  - ○ If off, leave off. Do not attempt to power them on or unlock.

Additional Resources

- **NICE Cybersecurity Workforce Framework - First Responder Roles:**
  https://www.nist.gov/itl/applied-cybersecurity/nice/nice-cybersecurity-workforce-framework
- **SearchSecurity: Computer Forensics First Responder Guide:**
  https://searchsecurity.techtarget.com/Computer-Forensics-First-Responder-Guide

Part 2

In the next chapter, we'll cover more advanced situations first responders might encounter, the concept of volatile vs. non-volatile data, and additional precautions for safety and evidence integrity.

First Responders' Guide to Evidence Collection, Part 2

Let's go deeper into some trickier situations, and the crucial concept of data volatility!

Understanding Data Volatility

This means how easily data is lost if not handled correctly. First responders need a basic grasp of this:

- **Volatile Data:** Lost when the device loses power.
  - **RAM Contents:** Running programs, network connections, some system state.
  - **Some OS Artifacts:** May exist only in memory until the machine is shut down.
- **Non-Volatile Data**
  - **Stored on Hard Drives/SSDs:** Files (even deleted ones), much of the system logs.
  - **Phones/Tablets Internal Storage:** Similar to the above, but the retrieval process can be more complex.

Why Volatility Matters to You

It dictates the urgency:

1. **If You Must Shut Down:** Prioritize volatile data capture if specially trained and tools are available. This might involve a quick 'triage' image of RAM, or detailed notes about what was displayed on-screen.
2. **If You Can Preserve Power State:** With powered-on machines, the focus shifts to careful network isolation, photography, and awaiting the forensic specialists.

Challenging Scenarios

Let's look at a few situations that demand extra caution:

- **Servers:** Rarely should these be powered down by non-specialists. Often, preserving running system state for analysis is critical, and a hasty shutdown can damage data or make analysis harder. Seek expert help ASAP.

- **Encryption:** If the device is secured with full-disk encryption, your options become very limited. If possible, keep it powered on, isolated, and obtain either technical assistance to attempt a live decryption or court-authorized passwords.
- **Remote Wiping:** Some sophisticated suspects have software to delete incriminating data remotely. Immediate network isolation at the firewall/router level *might* be possible, but will likely need specialists.
- **Anti-Forensics:** Deliberate attempts to mislead investigators with false timestamps, booby-trapped files… tread carefully. One odd file could be a trigger to wipe the drive. Suspect this if there's evidence of technical skill on the part of the user.

Incident Response Beyond the Technical

First responders sometimes have duties beyond pure evidence preservation:

- **Personnel Safety:** Are there suspects still on the scene? Is the situation hazardous (chemical spills, etc.) in a way that impacts your safety around electronic devices?
- **Witness Interviews:** Even if not your main job, be observant. Early witness statements about how the person used the computer can offer valuable investigative leads later.
- **Physical Evidence Correlation:** Documenting non-digital traces can be important. Was there a half-written note next to the PC, printouts of sensitive documents, or unusual tools?

Chain of Custody: It Starts With You

- **What Is It?:** A meticulous log of who had access to the evidence, where it was stored, what actions were performed, and all of this in chronological order.
- **Why It's Critical:** If this log has gaps, or improper procedures were followed, evidence may be rendered inadmissible in court, no matter how incriminating it seems!

- **Your Role:** Start a chain of custody form THE MOMENT you touch the device. Note date, time, location, your name, justification for your actions, serial numbers of the evidence… be thorough!

Additional Resources

- **NIST Computer Forensic Reference Data Sets (CFReDS):** (https://www.cfreds.nist.gov/) – Contains resources for training first responders on digital evidence handling
- **IACIS (International Association of Computer Investigative Specialists) - Has training for law enforcement first responders:** (https://www.iacis.com/)

Wrapping Up

The actions of first responders can significantly impact the success of a digital forensic investigation. By understanding basic principles, acting cautiously to preserve the scene, and realizing when to call in the experts, you become an invaluable asset to ensuring justice is served.

Conclusion

Throughout this book, we've embarked on a journey through the essentials of Computer Forensics. You've moved from simply *using* computers to peering behind the curtain at the rich and sometimes shadowy world of digital evidence. Let's recap the major milestones:

- **The Building Blocks:** You now understand how data is represented – from the simple bit to hashes that ensure file integrity, and even the intricacies of hexadecimal for when you need to go truly low level.
- **Hardware & Software Dance:** Exploring hard drives, file systems, and the ways operating systems meticulously log activities gave you the tools to understand the structure of digital storage.
- **The Forensic Process:** From using hardware probes for secure copying, through the careful creation of forensic images, to the integration of evidence from multiple sources – you grasp the core workflow of an investigator.
- **Searching the Depths:** Mounting images, understanding the wealth of clues hidden in system logs, and using forensic tools to create timelines have equipped you for methodical analysis in the search for truth.
- **Where It All Begins** Recognizing the importance of first responders in preserving a digital crime scene, and the special considerations for various device types showcases how everyone plays a role in ensuring justice prevails.

The Road Ahead

Computer forensics is a field of constant change. Criminals evolve their techniques, technologies advance, and laws adapt. Here's how to stay ahead of the curve:

- **Ongoing Learning:** Forensic blogs, conferences like those run by SANS Institute, and additional training courses will help you keep up with the latest tools and methodologies.
- **Specialization:** Did a specific area spark an intense interest? Mobile device forensics, network forensics, recovering data from damaged drives – there are whole worlds of specialization within our field.
- **The Human Factor:** Remember, digital investigations are ultimately about people. Developing your understanding of cybercrime psychology and the legal side of investigations will make you a more well-rounded digital detective.

The Power (and Responsibility) of Digital Forensics

The ability to uncover evidence hidden within our devices is a potent tool. With that power comes the following responsibilities:

- **Ethics Stand Above All:** With access to deeply personal or highly sensitive data, maintaining integrity and avoiding bias is paramount.
- **Upholding the Law:** A forensic analyst works within the boundaries of legal search warrants, data privacy concerns, and proper procedures to ensure evidence remains admissible.
- **The Pursuit of Truth:** Whether it's exonerating the innocent or building a compelling case against the guilty, your findings have real-life consequences. Take pride in the meticulous process that leads to them.

A Final Word

I hope this book has not only opened your eyes to the fascinating world of digital forensics, but also instilled a sense of the profound impact this field has on our society. Whether you pursue this as a career or simply gain a better understanding of how digital traces factor into our lives, may you use your new knowledge wisely and always in the service of justice.

Farewell, for now!